AN EMPTY WAGON MAKES A LOT OF NOISE

AN EMPTY WAGON MAKES A LOT OF NOISE

A Collection of Memorable Sayings and Expressions

Sherrill C. Dunbar

To order additional copies of this book, contact:
Xlibris Corporation
1-888-795-4274
www.Xlibris.com
Orders@Xlibris.com
51621

CONTENTS

This book is dedicated to my family.

It's okay to give your children some of the things you didn't have, but don't forget to give them some of the things you did have.

Church Bulletin

Acknowledgement

This book contains a collection of some memorable sayings and expressions that many individuals and I remember hearing frequently during our childhood. We heard them from our parents, grandparents, aunts, uncles, teachers, neighbors and others in the various communities where we grew up. These sayings represent words that were often spoken to teach us a lesson or make a point. The power and influence of these words are captured in the personal reflections interwoven between the chapters of this book. I am truly thankful to everyone who contributed to this book and, most of all, to God for all His blessings.

Words Of Caution

God sees everything.
This is a reminder that God is everywhere and God sees everything all the time even when you think no one is watching or when you're doing something you shouldn't be doing.

God don't like ugly.
These words are spoken to someone who does something mean-spirited or deceitful.

Be careful what you pray for.
Be careful what you ask for.
These are words of caution. Sometimes you may desire to have a material item that someone else has. However, you need to be careful because you don't know what the person went through to get the item or is going through to maintain it.

If you play with fire, you'll burn.
This means that you suffer the consequences of your actions. "Fire" represents something that could potentially hurt or harm you.

Everything that shines isn't gold.
Don't take things at face value.

Let sleeping dogs lie.

Don't try to change circumstances that are beyond your control.

What you do in the dark will come out in the light.
If it don't come out in the wash, it'll come out in the rinse.

When you think you've gotten away with something you should not have done, beware! Sooner or later someone will find out exactly what you did.

Feed him/her off a long handle spoon.

This means to approach a person with caution.

Everyone who smiles in your face is not your friend.

These are words of caution. Don't assume that everyone who laughs with you or talks to you is your friend.

All dogs bite.

You can't trust everyone you know so watch out!

Every Shut Eye Ain't Sleep And Every Goodbye Ain't Gone

When I was growing up, my daddy would always say, "Every shut eye ain't sleep and every goodbye ain't gone." For a long time I didn't know what he was talking about. I finally figured out that this means to be careful when you're bad mouthing someone because the person being talked about can be near you without your knowledge and can hear what you're saying. Now I find myself telling my children this saying and some other ones. (Sandra M. McKie)

Don't Take Any Wooden Nickels

Before I left home to go to college, my mom gave me some advice for dealing with college and campus life. While we discussed many things, I remember her saying, "Marvin, don't take any wooden nickels from anybody." My mom's dad had given her the same advice when she was a young girl. This expression was my mom's way of telling me not to accept everything someone offered me, and to stay away from quick fixes and things that sounded too good to be true. Her words encouraged me to focus on my lessons and develop a hard work ethic that I have carried into everything I do. (Marvin Jeffcoat)

Words For Children

Everybody don't live here.
What you say to a child who wants to do what "everybody else" is doing. For example, when a child comments that everybody else is doing something such as going to the movies or wearing a certain kind of clothing, a parent or adult can respond by saying, "Everybody don't live here."

Don't get too big for your britches.
What an adult says to a child who is trying to act grown.

God don't like ugly.
This is told to a child who misbehaves or is disobedient. Just hearing the word "God" is enough to make most children straighten up because no one wants to do anything to disappoint God.

Use your head for something other than a hat rack.
In other words, use your mind!

Your eyes are bigger than your stomach.
This is said to a child who doesn't eat all of the food he/she asked for.

You got the big eyes.

This is said to a child who wants and asks for something he/she doesn't need.

You stepped out of time.

You're stepping out of time.

You're getting beside yourself.

This is said to a child who disrespects or talks back to an adult.

A hard head makes a soft behind.

A hard-headed child does not do what his/her parents asks or does not follow parental advice and instructions. Hard-headed children usually receive many spankings. The more spankings a child receives, the softer her/his behind becomes. Hence, "a hard head makes a soft behind."

The chip don't wander too far from the block.

This means that a child has the same traits, mannerisms, and personality as one parent or both parents.

You're itching for a whipping.

This saying applies to a child who continuously misbehaves after repeated warnings from a parent or another adult, and it means that the child is going to get a spanking if his/her behavior continues.

Keep living.

The longer you live, the more you will experience and learn.

I brought you in this world and I'll take you out.

This is a parent's way of telling a child not to disrespect him/her again.

Don't let dark catch you.

Don't let the sundown catch you still in the street.

Be home before it gets dark outside.

Crying never hurt anybody.

You can cry until you cry blood.

You can cry until the cows come home.

You can cry as long as you want.

You're trying to be a big wheel but you can't do your own rolling.

This applies to a child who is trying to be an adult when he/she isn't ready for the responsibilities that come with adulthood.

Children should be seen and not heard.

This describes how children should behave especially around adults. When adults are having a conversation, a child should behave and be seen but the child should not interrupt the adults.

I'll whip you into next week.

I'll whip you 'til you rope like okra.

This means that you are going to get a spanking that you'll never forget!

I Want To Hear A Rat Pee On Cotton

When my mother wanted her kids to be very quiet, she would say, "I want to hear a rat pee on cotton." As a small child, I never knew why she referred to rats peeing on cotton (and I never asked), but I knew it meant absolute silence. Some years later when I was in college, I was playing a card game of Spades in the student center. On this particular day, my partner and I were taking a terrible beating—we had negative points while our opponents only needed two or three books to win the game. Suddenly one of the women we were playing against looked up and said, "You guys don't have much to say when you're losing." The other woman replied, "Yeah, they're so quiet you can hear a rat pee on cotton."

I immediately thought back to how my mother used to order my siblings and me to be quiet, and for the first time I tried to imagine how quiet it would have to be to actually hear a rat pee on cotton. I began to laugh uncontrollably and couldn't finish the card game. That night I called my mother and asked her why she used that phrase when she wanted her kids to be quiet. My mom told me she never thought about the phrase but she remembered her mother using it when she wanted silence in the house. However, when my mother was younger, hearing the phrase was more like a game. Her mother would place a hand to her ear and say, "Listen, I can hear the rats peeing on cotton." My mother, her brothers and sisters would stop what they were doing and listen for the sound of rats peeing (they grew up on a farm and cotton was one of my grandfather's crops). As my mother and her siblings grew older, my grandmother would yell, "I want to hear a rat pee on cotton," and they knew to be quiet! (James Douglas)

Lessons From School

When I was a young child just about everyone around me including teachers used different sayings and expressions to teach a lesson. Here are some sayings I remember learning at school:

-If a task is once begun, never leave it 'til it's done;
Be the labor great or small, do it well or not at all. (Author unknown)
<u>Lesson</u>: When you start a task, complete it and do it well.

-What we do here, what we say here, when you leave here, let it stay here. (Author unknown)
<u>Lesson</u>: Don't tell other people what's going on inside your house. (Thelma Phillips Jeffcoat)

Words About Relationships

Treat people like you want to be treated.
This is a restatement of the Golden Rule: "Do unto others as you would have them do to you."

You don't miss your water until your well runs dry.
You don't miss someone until she/he is no longer around. Also, you don't miss something until you no longer have it.

Kill them with a smile.
"Them" refers to people who don't like you. When you're around someone who doesn't like you SMILE. Your happy attitude is likely to upset the person.

Don't beat a man when he's down.
When a person is experiencing some type of difficulty, don't do anything that will contribute to the person's situation.

If you lie down with dogs, you'll get up with fleas.
Others will judge you based on your friends and associates.

He may be sanctified but he ain't satisfied.

These words apply to an individual who says he/she is saved and has put his/her worldly ways behind. However, the person's actions show that he/she is still engaging in the lusts/things of the world.

Don't let the devil take the "j" out of your joy.

Don't let others do or say anything to take away your happiness.

Why should a man buy the cow when he can get the milk free?

In other words, why should a man make a commitment to a promiscuous woman who is willing to live with him and engage in premarital sexual relations?

If you give a dog a bad name, people will throw stones at it.

A "bad name" represents a bad reputation. Most people don't want to associate with someone who has a bad reputation.

Every rat has more than one hole; every hole has more than one rat.

This saying describes a situation where spouses are cheating on each other.

My Granddaddy Said

During my childhood, my granddaddy always knew what to say to make me feel better or help me with a problem. He could also explain something complex in very simple terms. Because of this, I thought he was a phenomenal person who carried some sort of special power that allowed him to do supernatural things. When I was a young girl, I often heard him make "coded" statements that, at the time, made absolutely no sense to me. Now that I'm an adult, I have learned what some of the statements actually meant. Here are a few of his statements and my interpretation of them:

"I'd rather drink muddy water and sleep in a hollow log." <u>Interpretation</u>: He used this statement to communicate his preference not to do something.

"I will go to a bear fight with a switch." <u>Interpretation:</u> He loved me so much that he would take on King Kong unarmed in order to protect me.

"I look through muddy water and see dry land." <u>Interpretation:</u> This statement was a testament to the strength of his faith and his ability to see beyond difficult situations.

"Your hand is so good I am going to throw mine in and take yours." <u>Interpretation:</u> You are blessed and I would like to trade places with you. (Stella H. Taylor)

Man May Appoint But
God Can Dis-appoint

Sometimes when I think of my mother, I recall the many expressions she often used to make a point. One that I can't get out of my mind is hearing her say, "Man may appoint but God can dis-appoint." I was a teenager the first time she spoke these words to me. Over the years I learned that this was her way of telling me that throughout life people will make plans for me, direct me to do things, or appoint me for certain positions. However, those plans and things will change if they are not part of God's master plan for me. (Donna W. Matthews)

Words Dealing With Conversations

Larose catch Melrose.

Mind your own business. Whenever a nosey person tries to find out what you and someone else are talking about say, "Larose catch Melrose" to the person.

If you don't have anything nice to say, keep your mouth shut.

If you cannot say anything nice about someone then don't say anything at all.

A hit dog will bark.
A hit dog will bark the loudest.

A guilty person will either speak first or speak the loudest.

A dog that brings a bone will take a bone.

A person who will share a lie or rumor with you will also spread a lie or rumor about you. If you engage in gossip with another person, you can be sure that after your conversation the person will take something you said and spread a rumor about you.

Don't beat around the bush.
Spare me the pain and bring me the baby.

In other words, get to the point! When engaged in a conversation, don't add a lot of extraneous and irrelevant information.

Squat this rabbit and jump another one.

Change the subject.

Don't hang your dirty laundry for others to see.

Don't share your household business with others.

Hum To Confuse The Devil

My grandmother is an old sage – full of wisdom and knowledge. One day I was talking to her about some things that were not going well for me. I told her that it seemed like every time a good thought came to my mind something negative countered the thought. My grandmother then said, "That's because the devil hears your thoughts, and if he can he will thwart them. Chile, you have to hum to confuse the devil." I thought about what she said and decided it couldn't hurt to hum, so I did. After a while, things did seem to get better for me. I know God had a major hand in the situation but I also like to think my grandmother was right. I still hum today whenever my mind is busy. (Linda Blake)

Go Put Some Looks On

Whenever my mom saw me looking unkempt she would say, "Go put some looks on." This was her way of telling me to make myself more physically attractive by combing my hair, washing my face, putting on make-up or doing whatever was needed to improve my appearance. (Teresa Chappell)

Words About Commitment

If the shoe don't fit, don't wear it.
If you can't do the job or task, don't pretend that you can.

Don't bite off more than you can chew.
Don't let your mouth write a check that your body can't cash.
Don't take on more than you can reasonably do. In other words, don't over commit yourself.

[You have] Too many irons in the fire.
This means you're doing more tasks than you can handle.

Your word is your bond.
Act on what you commit to because this builds character.

God Bless The Child That Has Its Own

Often when I was alone with my mother she would say, "God bless the child that has its own." She would also say, "I'm going to tell you what my parents told me. Mama may have and Papa may have, but God bless the child that has its own." Hearing these words throughout my childhood encouraged me to strive to acquire my own worldly goods. With the encouraging words from my mother, I was determined to get an education, acquire my own worldly goods, and help others by encouraging them. I now encourage my two sons to think about tomorrow, strive to become independent, and make a life for themselves. (Cynthia James Scott)

God Is Talking To You

I recall that whenever there was a thunderstorm, my siblings and I had to be quiet and be still. We could not talk, laugh, run, jump, play or move. This was the "house" rule whenever there was a storm. My grandmother would always comment that thunderstorms are God's way of talking to us. We continued this habit of being quiet and still even when we became adults. One day I was at a sister's house when there was a severe thunderstorm in her area. Since I couldn't do much, I decided to be quiet and still by taking a nap. Before I fell asleep, I heard my sister instruct her son (who was about four years old) to stop playing with his toys and sit on the sofa with her. After listening to the sound of thunder for a while, my nephew asked, "Mama, why does it keep thundering?" My sister, remembering what she had been told as a child, said, "Because God is talking to us." At that moment, we heard a loud sound of lightening crackling in the sky. Then my nephew, in the innocence of a child, said, "Mama, why does God have to talk so loud?" (Sherrill C. Dunbar)

Words About Staying Focused

A jack-of-all-trades and master of none.
This saying describes a person who is familiar with a lot of different things but is not skilled in any one thing or is not able to do anything well.

An empty wagon makes a lot of noise.
This refers to someone who attempts to speak intelligently about a specific subject or issue but does not have the knowledge, understanding or depth needed to do so.

Running around like a dog chasing its tail.
Running around like a chicken with its head cut off.
When a chicken's head is cut off, the chicken runs around aimlessly and doesn't know where it is going. When a dog chases its tail, the dog runs around in a circle over and over again. These expressions are used to describe someone who doesn't have clear thoughts or a well-defined plan for accomplishing a task.

Where there's a will, there's a way.
As long as you have the will power and desire to accomplish a task, you will overcome the obstacles preventing you from reaching your goal.

It's a poor dog that won't wag his own tail.
It's a sorry dog that won't scratch its own fleas.
This means to " toot your own horn" by talking and telling others about your accomplishments because no one else will do it for you. Most people are more likely to talk about your failures than your accomplishments.

An idle mind is the devil's workshop.
An idle mind is one that is not being used for good and constructive purposes. It conjures up deceitful thoughts that can lead to trouble.

Keep it in the middle of the road.
This means to always use good judgment and discretion.

You can lead the mule to the water but you can't make him drink.
This means that even though you give or equip a person with all the resources needed to accomplish a task, you cannot force the person to take the first step or necessary actions to accomplish the task.

A rolling stone gathers no moss.
A rolling stone is a person who is focused and goal-oriented. This person constantly works towards achieving his/her goals, and does not have time to engage in idle conversation, foolishness and other distractions.

Be Your Own Wheel

I grew up in a family with two sisters and no brothers. Since I was the only male child in my family, I spent a lot of time with my father. Even though my father had very little formal schooling, he had a great deal of practical common sense. He also was ingenious at figuring things out and getting things done. When I was about 10 years old, my father would often say, "Son, to be your own wheel you must be able to do your own rolling." He frequently said this to me as he and I worked weekends in a landscaping service he started and operated as a side business. At first I didn't really think much about what he was saying to me. However, as I grew older I realized that this was his way of telling me that to be truly independent and self-sufficient, I had to be willing to assume personal responsibility and accountability for whatever I wanted to pursue. This advice has been useful to me throughout my life, and I have even shared it with my son. (Johnnie Earl Barnes)

Are Your Ducks In Order

My grandfather was the first African American to receive a doctorate degree in biology from the University of Mississippi. He had a long, illustrious career at Mississippi Valley State University in Itta Bena, Mississippi. While there, he held several positions including Chair of the Biology Department, Dean of Academics, and professor. Despite being a highly educated person, my grandfather often explained daily life by sprinkling his speech with expressions symbolic of his rural upbringing. Shortly before I graduated from high school, I remember him asking me if my ducks were in order. I had no idea what he was referring to, and I reminded him that I didn't own any ducks. He patiently explained to me that he was asking if I had completed all requirements and had everything in order so I could graduate. When I'm unorganized at work or home, I recall my grandfather's expression and tell myself that my ducks are not in order when they need to be. (Tina Smith Younger)

Words About Self

The pot can't call the kettle black.
The margarine can't talk about the butter.
Don't say something negative about someone when what you're saying also applies to you.

Those in glass houses must not throw stones.
Don't spread gossip about the problems going on in someone else's house when you are having the same problems in your house.

I gotta see a man about a dog.
I gotta see a man about a mule.
When someone wants to know where you're going, this is a polite way of saying none of your business.

Sweep around your own back door before you try to sweep around mine.
Take care of the problems in your own house before you try to take care of the problems in someone else's house.

You made your bed, now lie in it.
This means you have to live with the negative consequences of your actions.

Give Your Heart To God

Before I started the first grade, my mama sat me down and talked to me about acceptable and unacceptable behavior. I was six years old at the time so I don't remember everything she told me that day. I do recall, however, that during the conversation she looked at me sternly and said, "If I get a call at my j-o-b about y-o-u, you're gonna give your heart to God and your behind to me." Even though I was a young child, I had enough sense to know that I needed to behave at school. Hearing my mama tell me this saying became a ritual the first day of every school year through my senior year of high school. Needless to say, my mama never got a call at her j-o-b about m-e! (Katrina Hart Lorick)

You Must Have A Hole In Your Head

Sometimes before my mama left to go to the store or somewhere else, she'd tell me to wash the dishes or mop the floor. Without her saying so, I knew she wanted me to have my chores done by the time she returned home. If she came home and saw that I hadn't done everything that I was supposed to do, she'd call me into the room and say, "Boy, you must have a hole in your head." To her, this was the only thing that could explain why I hadn't finished my chores! (Leroy Henry)

Words About Physical Attributes

Don't nothing want a bone but a dog.
This means that a man is not attracted to skinny women.

Beauty is skin deep but ugly is to the bone.
Don't judge a person by her/his outward appearance only. A person who is physically attractive may have a bad personality. However, someone who is less attractive physically may be a very caring person with a pleasant personality.

The darker the berry, the sweeter the juice.
These are words to show admiration for a dark-skinned person.

[You're] No bigger than a minute.
What you would say to someone who is skinny or very petite.

Slower than molasses.
This is used to describe someone who moves very slowly.

I heard you before you said a word.
You have formulated an opinion about a person based on his/her appearance, facial expressions, mannerisms, and other nonverbal cues.

Coffee Will Make You Black

During my childhood, I spent a lot of time at my maternal grandparents' house. My grandfather worked during the day, so I didn't get to spend as much time with him as I did with my grandmother. However, whenever he was home I would observe him and take note of what he did. I remember that my grandfather drank coffee a lot. He didn't put any milk or cream in his coffee but he did use a little sugar. When I was a young child I would ask him for some coffee, but he would never give me any. He would always say, "You can't have any 'cause coffee makes you black." As a young child, I thought this was true because my grandfather was a very dark-skinned man! (Sherrill C. Dunbar)

Daddy's Stories

My father was born in a small southern community and grew up there during the early 1900s. Whenever I complained about something, he would tell me a story about how far he had to walk to school each day. He told me the story so many times that I knew it by heart and could even recite it by the time I turned twelve.

According to my father, each day he walked somewhere from 10 to 15 miles to get to school (He increased the number of miles as I grew older). He made this long walk to school, even in frigid temperatures. The frequent walking put many holes in his shoes and tore them. Since he couldn't afford to buy another pair of shoes, he tied his worn shoes with string to keep them on his feet. Other children laughed at him but he didn't care. He was determined to get an education.

My father also told me that his Grandmama Lucinda would always take him to the general store with her (that was another 10-mile walk) because he could read and count money. Since Grandmama Lucinda could neither read nor write she depended on my father to help her purchase monthly supplies and tell her if the white storekeeper was cheating her out of her money. My father would count Grandmama Lucinda's money and tell her how much to give the white storekeeper. If the storekeeper owed Grandmama

Lucinda some change from her purchase, she would always show my father the change and ask him if she had received the correct amount.

As a young child and teenager, I didn't understand how these stories had anything to do with my particular problems. It was generally the same stories for all of my problems and I wanted answers, not stories. When I became an adult, my ears and eyes were finally opened. My father gave me some powerful advice in his simple stories:

-If there is something in life that you seriously want or desire to do, you must be willing to work hard for it and not let obstacles stand in your way.

-If there is something you want to achieve, press on to accomplish it and never give up hope regardless of how difficult times may get.

-Each generation should work hard to move forward and improve on the accomplishments of the previous generation.

-Complaining doesn't accomplish anything.

(Fannie M. Bivins)

Other Sayings

A bird in your hand is worth more than two in the bush.
A bird in a hand is worth two in the bush.
Something that you own or can touch and hold is worth more than what someone promises to give you (always go with the sure thing).

The devil must be beating his wife.
This situation occurs whenever it rains while the sun is shining.

Jumping from the frying pan into the fire.
When you do something to make a bad situation worse, you have jumped from the frying pan into the fire.

You don't have a pot to piss in or a window to throw it out of.
This means you are poor.

If the good Lord's willing and the creek don't rise.
This means you will be at a designated place if the Lord wants you to be there and a natural disaster doesn't prevent you from arriving at the place.

There's more than one way to skin a cat.
There's more than one way to cook a chicken.
This means there is more than one way to complete a task.

Don't count your chickens before they hatch.

Don't spend what you don't have.

You must have eyes in the back of your head.

What you say to a person who tells you what you are doing even though the person isn't in the room with you or near you.

Fair to midland.

This is another way of saying that you're feeling well. For example, if someone asks "How are you today?" you could respond by saying "Fair to midland."

No matter how bad things are for you, there's always someone worse off.

Be thankful for your blessings.

You must've gotten up on the wrong side of the bed.

This is what you say to someone who wakes up in a bad mood or when things aren't going as planned.

You are working my nerves.

This is another way of saying you are testing my patience.

Sayings About Luck

Gray hair is a sign of good luck.

If you put hats on the bed or table, you'll have bad luck.

If you put your purse on the floor, you'll always be broke.

If you don't come in and go out of the same door, you'll have bad luck.

If you split a pole while walking with someone, you'll have bad luck.

If you sleep with shoes under your bed you'll have a restless night.

If a red bird comes to your porch then flies away less than ten seconds later, you're going to have bad luck. If the bird stays for more than ten seconds, you'll have good luck.

Sayings About Body Talk

If your right eye is jumping, you're going to have good luck.

If your left eye is jumping, you're going to have bad luck.

If the bottom of your foot itches, you're going someplace you've never been before.

When one of your ears itches, someone is talking about you.

If your right hand itches, you're going to get some money.

If your left hand itches, you're going to get some mail.

If your nose itches, someone is coming to visit you.

Sayings About Pregnancy

If you dream about fish, someone you know is pregnant.

If you dream about the birth of a baby, someone you know is going to die.

If you dream that a pregnant person will have a baby boy, the person will actually have a baby girl and vice versa.

If you swallow pumpkin seeds or watermelon seeds, you'll get pregnant.

If you carry a baby low, you're having a girl.

If your hips spread a lot during your pregnancy, you're having a boy.

If you carry a baby high, you're having a boy.